Development of Mosaic Flo

The earliest floor- and wall-mosaics replaced woven wall-hangings, rugs and carpets; many of their designs reproduced in stone the weave and patterns of textiles. Mosaics, with their simplicity and beauty, can be appreciated by everyone; they bring Roman sites to life in a way that buildings (little of whose superstructure often remains) rarely do, and they make it easy to visualise how life was actually lived in those times.

At Fishbourne, the polychrome mosaic of a cupid on a dolphin, laid in the second century AD, was designed as a large 'carpet' to be laid against a chequer-board surround; in front of the two doorways in this room there are even patterned 'doormats'. In the baths of the villa at Chedworth in Gloucestershire there are mosaic 'bathmats' with designs in *peltae* and interlacing circles. Similar mosaic mats and carpets can be found throughout the Roman world.

In the first century AD, Pliny noted that walls and vaulted ceilings were being decorated with mosaics, and in many cases *smalti*, or glass paste tesserae, were used to increase the brilliance of the design. Many such wall-mosaics can still be seen in Italy and there is little doubt that they were also made in Britain. Unfortunately only a handful of tesserae survives as evidence.

Mosaics have been used as a decorative medium on walls and columns for nearly 5000 years. In Iraq in about 3000 BC the walls of the sanctuary of Eanna at Urak (modern Warka) were decorated with coloured cones of baked clay. The cones were pressed into the mud brick walls until only

Above: *Artist's impression of a living-room at Fishbourne during the second century* AD. *The mosaic 'carpet' is set against a chequer-board surround of dark grey and white tesserae.*

Below: *Decorated half-columns from the sanctuary of Eanna at Urak dating from about 3000* BC. *As a method of wall-decoration, the Sumerian system of pressing prefabricated cones of baked clay into the mud plaster surface of the walls and columns of buildings has much in common with later wall-mosaics. In addition to being highly decorative, the cones helped to reinforce and protect the surface.*

their bases remained above the surface; the geometric pattern of triangles, lozenges and zigzags formed by the cones strongly resembled the pattern of woven textiles. This technique may have evolved out of a desire to replace woven wall-hangings with a more permanent decoration and, at the same time, to consolidate and strengthen the wall.

Tesserae, small squares cut from flat plates of stone and shell, date from the third millennium BC in Sumeria. At the Temple of Ninkhursag at Tel Al' Ubeid flat pieces of stone and mother-of-pearl were used to decorate the surface of wooden columns. The columns were coated with bitumen, and small copper loops on the back of the tesserae were pressed down into this adhesive. Some of the bitumen was allowed to flow between the edges of the individual tesserae and the emphasis lent to each tessera was an effective part of the design. Other walls in the temple at Al' Ubeid were decorated with a frieze of birds and animals cut from thin slabs of shell and limestone, and these composite inlays were set against an overall background of mosaic. This combination of stone and tile inlays with tesserae was used in Egypt in the second millennium BC, but the use of tesserae for mosaic decoration then lapsed for over a thousand years.

The earliest mosaic floors were made from water worn pebbles carefully selected for their size and colour. Simple cobble-stone floors have a long history, but the earliest decorative pebble floors date from the ninth century BC in Assyria; a pebble floor using three colour tones was laid at Gordion in Asia Minor in the eighth century BC. In the fifth century BC the first known representational mosaics appeared, at Olynthus, in northern Greece.

Right: *An important fourth-century mosaic found at Hinton St Mary, Dorset, in 1963 and now in the British Museum. The pavement is in two parts, linked by a rectangular panel decorated by overall* peltae. *In the western (upper) portion, a central roundel shows Bellerophon slaying the Chimera, a favourite legend of the triumph of good over evil. The eastern (lower) square is divided into a central roundel surrounded by four semi-circular panels, with quarter-circles in each corner. The central roundel contains a portrait of a beardless man with the Chi-Rho monogram behind his head and a pomegranate on each side. The identification of this bust with Christ is unquestionable, although it is unusual to find a holy portrait on a floor. This may be an example of a mosaic pattern for a dome or cupola being unwisely chosen for use on a floor. The four quarter-circles in the corners contain busts identified as the four evangelists.* *(See page 33.)*

Below: *The Rape of Ganymede. A fine fourth-century mosaic in the villa at Bignor, Sussex. According to Homeric legend, Ganymede was carried away by the gods to become the cup-bearer to Zeus. Later legends relate that Zeus himself, in the shape of an eagle, carried the boy away to Olympus. Ganymede is naked except for his cloak and boots and a Phrygian cap on his head. This legend was a popular theme elsewhere in the Roman Empire and its choice as a subject by the owner of the Bignor villa hints at more cosmopolitan tastes than usual. Adjacent panels in the same room depict six maenads, or dancing girls, with swirling veils.*

The Olynthus mosaics were made of light and dark coloured pebbles about the size of a fist set in a pale brown mortar. The figures were set in light stones against a background of darker pebbles, and the mortar was allowed to infiltrate between the pebbles. Once again, this deliberate definition of each individual stone is an important part of the design. Among the mosaics at Olynthus is the earliest known representation on a mosaic floor of a mythological scene. The mosaic dates from about 420 BC, and it shows Bellerophon, who is riding his winged horse, Pegasus, in the act of slaying the Chimera. This scene was popular in the ancient world, and it reoccurs 750 years later in mosaic floors found at Lullingstone, Kent, and Hinton St Mary, Dorset.

Smaller pebbles helped to create an illusion of muscular strength in human figures and animals, and at Pella, in Macedonia, pebbles less than 10 mm in diameter were used. The transition from tiny pebbles to manufactured tesserae was natural, and it took place gradually after the fourth century BC. At first, pebbles were chipped into tiny pieces and used

Below: *Pebble mosaic from Pella in Macedonia, dating from the fourth century* BC. *This floor-mosaic, signed by the Greek artist Gnosis, is made up of carefully selected pebbles, often half an inch or less in diameter. At Pella, the mosaicists often inserted strips of lead to emphasise the outline of the figures. The practice probably originated as an aid in setting out the design, but the strips were frequently left in place after the mosaic was completed to heighten the dramatic contrast between the darker background and the lighter figures.*

only in areas where greater detail was needed, while the main ground of the floor was worked in natural pebbles. Later it appears to have proved more economical to prepare rectangular rods of stone from which individual tesserae could be cut as required.

The change from natural pebbles to tesserae of stone, baked clay and glass, provided a whole new range of colours for the mosaicist and led to subtle renderings of drapery and human and animal forms. The flat surfaces of tessellated floors were ground smooth, and such polishing enhanced the colour of the stones and increased the importance of careful colour gradation.

During the second century BC this fashion spread throughout the Hellenistic world, and on the island of Delos the houses of wealthy merchants were richly decorated with elaborately worked polychrome motifs set as *emblemata* against a background of coarser tesserae. By 80 BC these designs had reached Rome and the Temple of Fortuna at Palestrina was richly decorated with floor-mosaics, including a detailed

Below: *Three examples of black and white mosaics from Ostia, dating from the second and third centuries* AD. *This economic and disciplined style of mosaic work developed and flourished in Italy, where it became popular for use in public buildings. The figures are of black tesserae set as silhouettes against a white background. Fluid lines of white tesserae are used to model muscles and drapery. The winged sea-horses on the second-century floor at Fishbourne (see page 29) are executed in a similar style.*

scene of the river Nile which must surely have been laid by craftsmen from Alexandria.

At the beginning of the Christian era a new type of mosaic appeared in Italy, one that was very different from the polychrome representational mosaics derived from the Hellenistic world. On the Roman monochrome floors only black and white tesserae were used, and the figure or geometric shape was usually in black stones set into a background of white tesserae. Many of the floors at Pompeii and Herculaneum were decorated in this style in the first century AD, and the style was still in use in the second and third century at Ostia. These black and white floors contrast strongly with the polychrome floors which continued to be popular throughout the Roman Empire. Whereas the polychrome floors relied on chromatic shading to translate the art of the painter into stone, the new black and white mosaics depended entirely upon shape and the use of lines of white tesserae to create an impressionistic art form.

Although mosaic decoration on walls and floors had such a long history in the Mediterranean and the Near East, the craft was completely unknown in northern Europe before the Roman conquest. In the wake of the Roman army, however, came new ideas in architecture, town planning and interior decoration; the use of mosaics to decorate floors and walls spread gradually throughout the Empire from North Africa to Britain, and from Spain to the Black Sea.

Right: *The head of Venus. Detail of a fourth-century floor in the villa at Bignor, Sussex. A well executed but rather heavily restored mosaic in the* triclinium *of the villa features the delicate head of Venus. The goddess is nimbed and wears a diadem on her head. Her hair falls loosely and gracefully about her shoulders. This mosaic is clearly the work of a master craftsman.*

Below: *A wall-mosaic from the House of Neptune at Herculaneum.*

Mosaic Materials

Marbles and stones of many kinds were used throughout the Roman world for the manufacture of tesserae. Generally the mosaicist was supplied with local stone, but if imported marble was available (perhaps on a nearby site), he would often increase his range of colour with offcuts and rejected pieces.

In Britain most of the materials were indigenous, and a wide range of colours was available from the sedimentary rocks of southern England. Oolitic limestone and chalk were used for white tesserae, Lower Liassic rocks and Purbeck marble for varying shades of blue and grey. Sandstones and limestones gave shades of yellow, buff and brown, and in some areas red sandstone was also used. The borders surrounding mosaic floors were made of terracotta tile fragments cut to form red tesserae. In Roman Britain fragments of imported red glaze pottery (Samian ware from southern Gaul) were only rarely used and glass tesserae (*smalti*) were almost unknown, although common on the continent, particularly in wall-mosaics. On the mosaic depicting the four seasons excavated at Dyer Street in Cirencester in 1849, red glass tesserae were used in the head-dress of Spring, and eight rare, gilt glass tesserae were found loose on the site of the Roman villa at Southwick in Sussex; they almost certainly derived from a wall-mosaic. It seems probable that they were imported from continental workshops.

At Fishbourne, many of the mosaics were made of hard white chalk tesserae and the geometric pattern was outlined in greyish-black tesserae cut from a silty Jurassic shale. A stone-mason's workshop where these two types of tesserae were made has been excavated at Norden Farm near Corfe Castle in Dorset. The workshop was active in the first century; since at this time very few floor-mosaics were being laid in Britain, it seems likely that tesserae were sent, together with supplies of marble, to decorate the Palace.

Other stones in the Fishbourne mosaic floors include a brownish-red sandstone, red brick, blue and grey Purbeck limestone and red and yellow siltstones from the Mediterranean. These siltstones were used at Fishbourne in relatively large quantities to decorate the floors and furniture in the Neronian proto-palace; either surviving offcuts were used to make the tesserae or else they were cut from material derived from the proto-palace.

The Cretaceous and Jurassic rock formations of south-east England provided most of the subtle shades of coloured stone required for Romano-British mosaic floors.

The Liassic rocks of the Lower Jurassic provided yellow and buff sandstones and also stones in varying shades of grey, blue and black. Some coloured sandstones from Triassic deposits were also used, but the vast amount of white stone used in mosaic floors was chalk from the extensive Cretaceous deposits of southern England and oolitic limestone from the Middle Jurassic.

Jurassic shale from Kimmeridge in Dorset was used for tesserae and floor tiles and this minor 'industry' probably developed as an offshoot of the flourishing shale-working industry which produced such luxury ornaments as bangles, bowls, trays and table-legs.

Jurassic limestone from the Purbeck beds in Dorset also provided varying shades of grey and blue.

The choice of natural stones, dependent for their colour on the mineral content of the rock, accounts for the fact that most mosaic floors when newly washed look as bright and as fresh today as they did when in use nearly two thousand years ago.

Left: *Head of 'Spring' from a 'four seasons' mosaic found in Corinium, Cirencester. The goddess wears a head-dress of flowers and leaves, made partly from glass tesserae which are comparatively rare in Romano-British mosaics.*

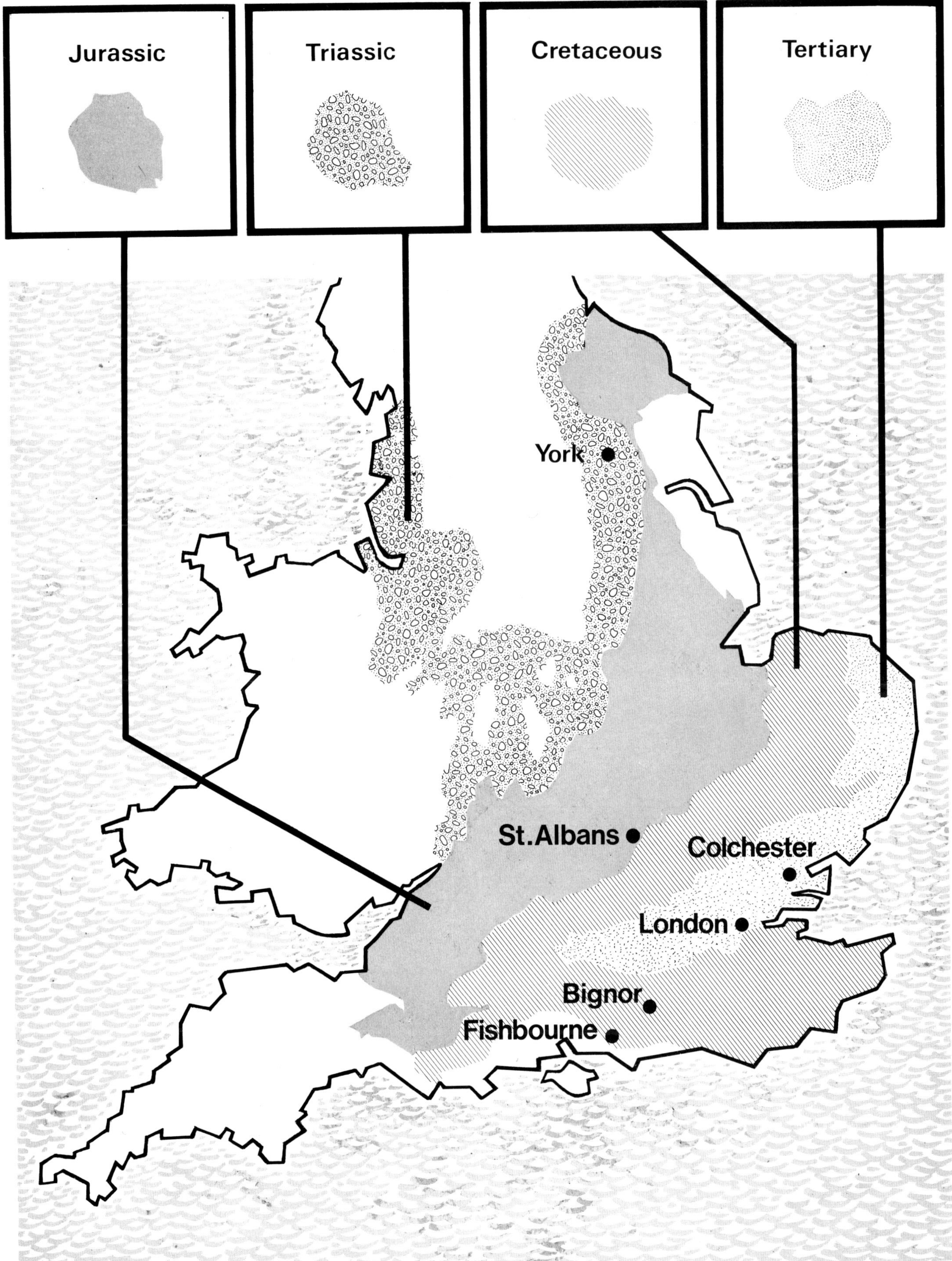
Jurassic
Triassic
Cretaceous
Tertiary
York
St. Albans
Colchester
London
Bignor
Fishbourne

Floors at Fishbourne · 1st generation

The floor-mosaics which decorated the Palace at Fishbourne at the end of the first century AD must have been laid by immigrant craftsmen brought to Britain for that purpose. They are the earliest surviving floor-mosaics in this country, although there were certainly earlier ones in the proto-palace built at Fishbourne in the late 60s, and also at the Roman villa excavated near Eccles in Kent and at the recently excavated baths in Exeter.

There were probably more than sixty floor-mosaics in the original Palace and major portions of a quarter of them survive today. The floors form an important, closely dated group and can be divided into two types.

The larger group is characterised by the domination of black and white geometric motifs, with only an occasional insertion of colour or floral motifs. Designs of this type were particularly popular in Italy and Gaul at this time, and although it is difficult to find exact parallels for any complete floor, many examples of floor-mosaics incorporating similar motifs can be seen at Pompeii and Herculaneum. The style continued to be used during the second century at Hadrian's Villa near Tivoli, east of Rome, and at the port of Ostia.

It is much more difficult to find parallels for the smaller group of polychrome floors, but the successful inclusion of sophisticated *guilloche* patterns and the careful use of colour indicates that craftsmen of the highest standard were employed.

Right: *An unusual polychrome floor-mosaic in room N21, constructed of red, white and blue/grey tesserae set against a black background. There are no close parallels for this mosaic, but the theme of four squares overlain by a central square used in room N3 appears again in this mosaic to create a linking background to the alternating central squares of red and blue/grey tesserae. The mosaicist has 'signed' this floor with a small diamond pattern of white tesserae inserted in the southern border.*

Below left: *A carefully laid black and white floor-mosaic in room N3 in the North Wing of the Palace. The simple and geometric design incorporates twenty-eight squares set against a simple linear framework. The squares contain a repetitive sequence of concentric squares enlivened by a pattern of four hollow squares overlain by a central square. This floor remained in use throughout the life of the building and it shows large areas of wear.*

Below: *The relatively unusual use of white tesserae set against a black background seen in room N21 is repeated here most effectively to depict this* cantharus, *or wine-cup, in a floor-mosaic at Ostia.*

Bottom: *Chequer-board design used as a 'door-mat' leading into room W6 in the West Wing. Simple squares of black and white tesserae form two rows of crosses.*

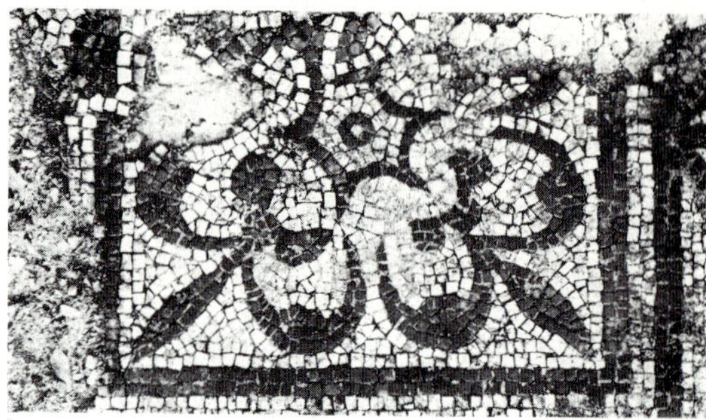

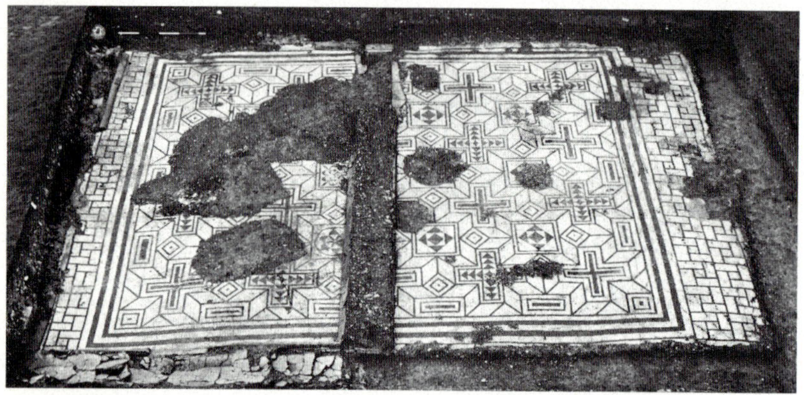

Top left: *An elaborate repetitive pattern of geometric motifs and light, square-shaped meanders set alternately against a background-linking meander design in room W3. In Gaul, all-over meanders occur on first- and second-century floor-mosaics at Bavay and Bous and individual meander motifs were used at Pompeii in the first century and at Ostia in the second century.*

Centre left: *One of the finest geometric floor-mosaics in the Palace. The repetitive pattern of crosses and false boxes covers an area of 513 sq. ft. Four rows of cross-shaped motifs are arranged between rows of squares and the framing pattern gives an illusion of boxes in perspective. Similar styles were popular at Pompeii, and many similar motifs can be seen at Hadrian's Villa east of Rome.*

Bottom left: *Contrasting styles in geometric mosaics in rooms N3 and N4. Compare the heavy effect of solid black and white squares and rectangles surrounded by wide bands of black tesserae with the light, airy effect of alternating square motifs set against a light linear framework.*

Top: *Floral motif in geometric mosaic in room N12. Three of the square panels in the southern half of this mosaic contain floral motifs, and it seems possible that all six of the southern panels once had similar motifs. The insertion of floral motifs into a geometric surround foreshadows the superb arabesque floral designs created at Hadrian's Villa in the following century. The northern part of this motif shows evidence of inferior repair during the Roman period.*

Above: *Simple geometric motif of black and white squares, set diagonally within each other, from the northern half of room N12.*

Top left: *A simple repetitive border pattern of overlapping rectangles in room N12. A similar design is used in room N19 as an overall pattern.*

Centre left: *Floor-mosaic in the Guest House of Hadrian's Villa near Rome. This second-century black and white mosaic has a central panel of floral arabesque, surrounded by panels of overlapping rectangles similar to the border of the floor-mosaic in room N12 at Fishbourne.*

Bottom left: *Black and white geometric floor-mosaic in the Guest House of Hadrian's Villa. The overall design has much in common with many of the designs used at Fishbourne sixty years before.*

Top: *Cross-shaped motif from the floor-mosaic in room N12. The infilling of solid triangles placed base to apex also occurs in the West Wing mosaic in room W6. The pattern around the cross is arranged to give an illusion of boxes and false perspective.*

Above: *Detail of a floor-mosaic in the House of the Grand Fountain at Pompeii. This pattern is very similar to the background meander in room W3 at Fishbourne.*

Top left: *The inner circle of rosettes and vine leaves surrounded by a well executed two-strand* guilloche.

Top right: *Polychrome mosaic in room N20, one of the finest floors in the first-century Palace. The carefully shaded colours and elaborate floral motifs which distinguish this floor seem not to have been used on other sites at this early date, although the overall plan of the floor, with concentric circular designs enclosed within a square, is found in the first century at Pompeii, Cividale and Brescello.*

The central panel wore out while the floor was in use. There is no evidence to suggest the nature of the central roundel, although a substantial portion of the surrounding circle of rosettes and leaves survives. There is no known parallel for this particular arrangement of rosettes and leaves.

The outer circle is filled with a polychrome two-strand guilloche *set against a black background. The twisted* guilloche *motif is rare in the first century and its construction required a high degree of technical competence from the mosaicist. The corners are filled with elaborate, well drawn designs incorporating* canthari *(wine cups) supported by tendrils, dolphins or fish. The combination of vases with fruit, and* canthari *with sprouting vine leaves, is common on Pompeian floor-mosaics and wall-paintings, but* canthari *linked with fish and dolphins are rarely seen.*

Centre left: *The individual rosettes and leaves were carefully constructed in shades of red, blue, yellow and white outlined in black and set against a white background.*

Bottom left: *Detail of the running scroll border in room W8. The simple design of tendrils and leaves has alternate nodes in yellow and red. Vine scrolls were frequently used to decorate the thresholds of Pompeian houses.*

Bottom right: *A well made black and white floor-mosaic in room W8 in the West Wing of the Palace. Many of the motifs are similar to those used in rooms N12 and N3; the unusual feature of this mosaic is its border panel of running scrolls and leaves combined with a highly stylised geometric pattern in the main area.*

The Mosaicist at work

The normal method of laying floor-mosaics in Roman Britain was by the 'direct' process. In this method the mosaicist set the tesserae into a slurry of hydrated lime and water poured over a semi-dry screed of crushed tile and lime mortar, supported by a rubble foundation. Occasionally, when mosaic floors have been lifted, it has been possible to detect 'setting-out' lines scratched into the surface of the mortar foundation. These would have been a great help to a mosaicist working by the 'direct' method.

In Greece and Italy it was possible to purchase prefabricated *emblemata* from mosaic workshops. These were set in position and the surrounding areas were filled with tesserae by the 'direct' process.

Below: *After the Roman Conquest, luxury goods and exotic building materials were imported into Britain in increasing quantities. At first, these imports were probably destined for military sites, but during the second half of the first century prestige public building was encouraged as part of a policy of Romanisation. In addition to building materials and exotic stones, architects, stone masons, artists and mosaicists must also have come to Britain to decorate the buildings being constructed at that time. There is evidence that Greek mosaicists worked in Italy, Spain, France and North Africa, and mosaicists with Roman names signed their work in Smyrna and Spain. It is not surprising, therefore, that we find evidence to suggest the use of immigrant artists in Britain during the first century.*

A mosaic floor from the 'Villa of Cicero' in Pompeii contains an *emblema* set in a marble tray and signed by the mosaicist Dioscurides of Samos. The complete tray, with the *emblema* on it, was set into the surrounding mosaic and the rim of the tray can still be seen.

The occurrence of standardised compositions and motifs on floors throughout the Roman Empire strongly suggests that 'copy-books' were used. These copy-books, drawn or painted on parchment, papyrus or wooden boards, were probably circulated from workshop to workshop throughout the Roman world in much the same way as a wallpaper catalogue is today. Such books would contain details of *emblemata* which were available ready-made, as well as detailed patterns of motifs which could be selected and arranged to the clients' individual requirements. Because of the perishable nature of such materials as wood and papyrus, no copy-books have survived, but it is thought that they were widely used.

It was suggested in 1930 that complex *emblemata* and elaborate pictorial floors might have been laid by the 'indirect' process. This technique, which is widely used today for modern mosaic work, involves laying the mosaic 'blind', unless a transparent backing material is used. The tesserae are set face down onto a suitable material with a water-soluble adhesive, and after the mosaic is set into position the backing material is removed.

There is little evidence for prefabricated *emblemata* in this country, but the obvious difference in quality between some of the major motifs on British floors and their surrounding panels and borders has led some people to suppose that they were not entirely unknown. A panelled floor laid at Verulamium (St Albans) in the second century was composed of sixteen panels which were almost certainly laid as *emblemata*. One of the panels was wrongly set at ninety degrees to its corresponding panel two rows away, and it seems that these panels were set 'blind' by the 'indirect' process. Once the floor is laid, this technique is virtually undetectable, unless the mosaicist has made a mistake, as he did at Verulamium. Sometimes, when a floor is lifted by archaeologists, it is possible to discern variations in the mortar beneath separate elements in the mosaic. At Hinton St Mary in Dorset dark, streaky mortar underlay the joins between prefabricated sections of a scroll, and this type of evidence is now sought whenever a mosaic floor has to be removed from its supporting matrix.

As the Province of Britain developed and the demand for mosaic floors grew, native artists and craftsmen began to try their hand at the new skill. The naive but lively 'Venus' floor from Rudston in Yorkshire, and the second century 'Medusa' floor from Fishbourne are both possible examples of local artists working in a new medium.

Little is known about how the mosaicists lived and worked; in rural areas they almost certainly lived in temporary accommodation close to the site, but it seems that in the fourth century centralised mosaic workshops were established in Britain. Master craftsmen from these workshops travelled around the country when commissioned by their clients, but a great deal of the preparatory stone-cutting would have been done at the central depot. Several heaps of used tesserae were found at Fishbourne and it is possible that these were stockpiled, either for repairing or relaying floors at Fishbourne, or possibly for resale as surplus material to be used on other sites.

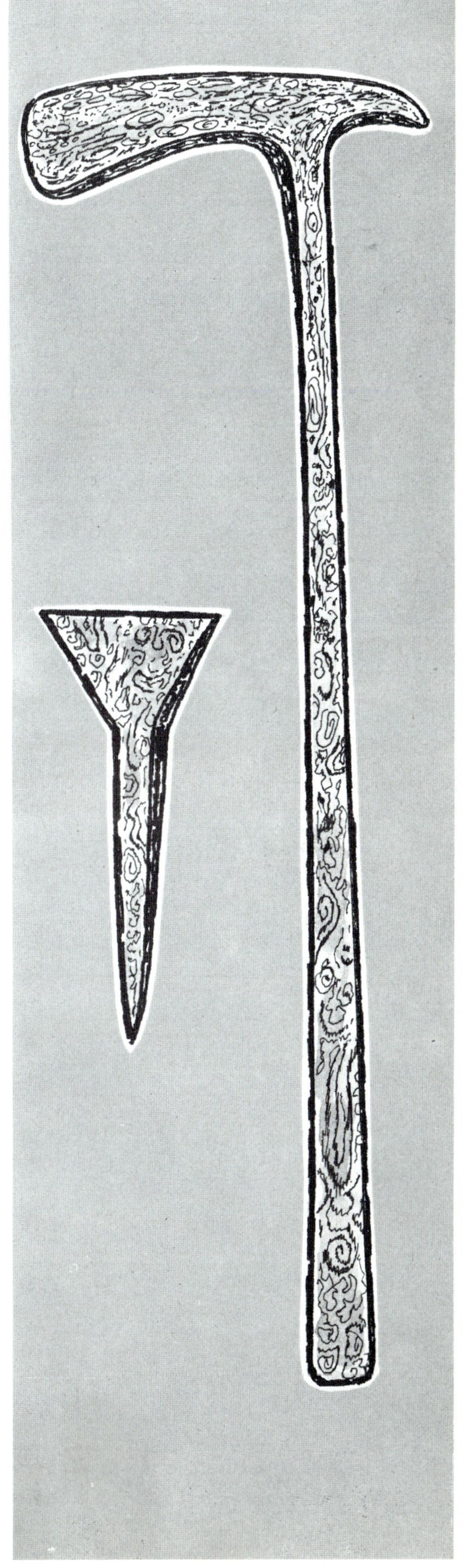

Right: *Mosaic worker's axe and chisel found on the site of the Roman town at Silchester.*

Left: *This section through the edge of a mosaic floor at Fishbourne shows the rubble foundation overlain by a bed of mortar. The tesserae are set in a thin lime slurry and they continue beneath the wall plaster up to the face of the stone wall. The quarter-round plaster which overlies the edge of the floor is a later addition.*

Below: *Vitruvius, writing in the first century* BC, *emphasised the importance of laying good foundations beneath a floor if it was to give satisfactory wear. He recommended a bedding layer of fist-sized stones covered by a thick layer of broken stones and lime. This layer was beaten and pounded by workmen to ensure that it was thoroughly consolidated before the floor was laid 'by rule and level'. Relatively few Romano-British floors were laid with the care described by Vitruvius, but most are laid on a carefully prepared lime mortar bed supported on a firm rubble foundation.*

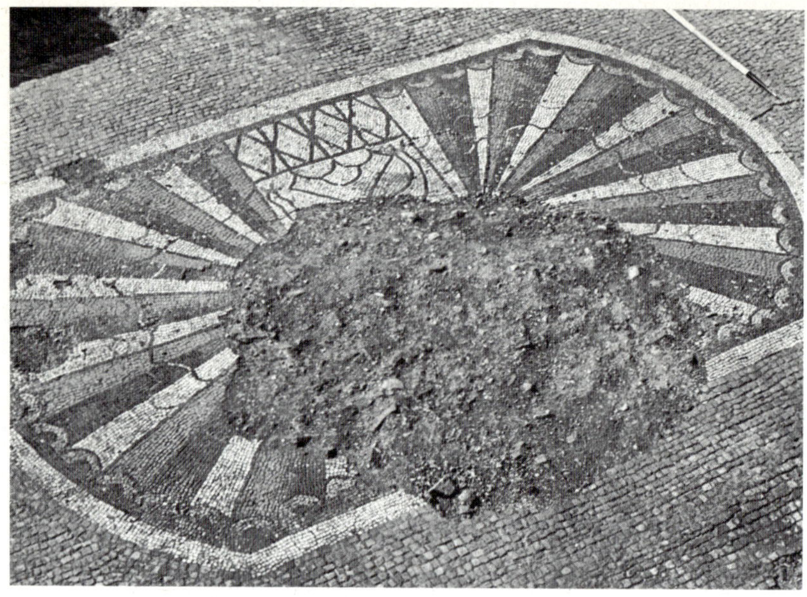

Room 5 – A mid-second-century mosaic, showing two scallop shells and the tails of two fish.

Room 7 – This was the main living-room during the second and third centuries. The small bird perched on a tendril in the northern border of the mosaic may be the mosaicist's 'trademark'.

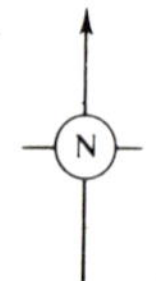

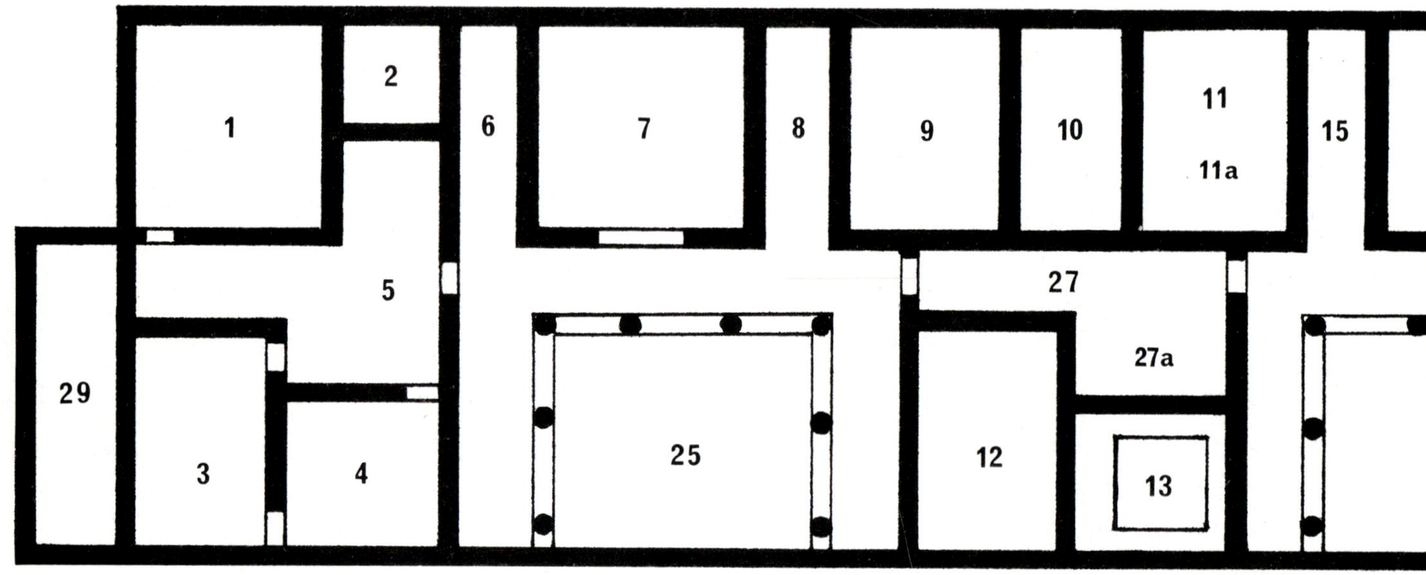

Room 3 – One of the earliest mosaics to be seen in Britain. At the south end of the wall, one of the few to survive, there is a blocked doorway which originally led into room 4.

Room 25 – The rooms in the North Wing were arranged around two small courtyards, each surrounded by a colonnade standing on large stone blocks, fronted by a stone gutter. Many of the original blocks are still in position around this courtyard, but the gutter blocks are modern reconstructions. The mass of tiles at the northern edge of the courtyard dates from the collapse of the roof during the third-century fire.

Room 12 – This was originally designed as one large unheated room which was divided into two during the second century. Several areas of the mosaic show patches of Roman repair.

Guide to the Mosaics in the North Wing

The complete expanse of the North Wing is housed under one roof and the north and south walls of the modern cover building were built on the line of the orginal Roman foundations. After the site had been abandoned at the end of the third century, many of the walls and their foundations were robbed for building stone and when the site was being conserved in 1967 it was necessary to fill the rubbish-filled robber trenches with a concrete agregate.

The rooms in the North Wing of the Palace are arranged as three separate suites around two small courtyard gardens (25 and 32). When the Palace was built in AD 75 all of these rooms had fine mosaic floors and substantial areas of six of these floors remain *in situ* today.

During the second and third centuries, many of the original mosaics were removed and replaced with more serviceable mortar and tessellated floors. Traces of the earlier floors can be seen underlying the hypocaust in room 1, the pink mortar floor in room 9, the tessellated floor in room 11 and the second-century mosaic in room 13.

Room 20 – A first-century polychrome mosaic, discovered when a water-main was laid across the site in 1961. The mosaic was re-excavated later that year, lifted and stored in a workroom for nearly six years before it was replaced exactly as it was found.

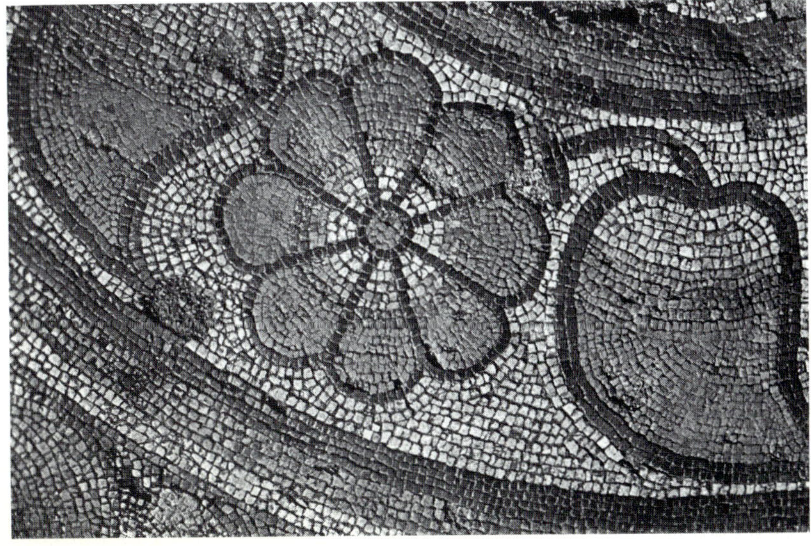

29. *Corridor with simple, hard-wearing tessellated floor dating from the second or third century.*

1. *An underfloor heating system was begun in this room, but was never completed. The idea was to heat the central chamber below the floor with hot air drawn through a central duct from a fire outside the building. Once the stone walls and the tile pillars were thoroughly heated, they would act as a heat storage unit and the furnace would only need occasional stoking. From the central chamber the hot air would have been drawn through four diagonal ducts to tile flues built into the walls of the room.*

2. *Fragments of a second- or third-century mosaic.*

4. *Like several other mosaics in the building, this floor was in use for about two hundred years. During that time areas of wear were patched with pink mortar. The remains of a large oven, which was built over the floor in the late second or early third century, can be seen in the south-east corner of the room.*

6. *A small heated room.*

8. *An early third-century mosaic with scallop shells in each corner and a central Solomon's Knot surrounded by vases and fish.*

27. *A tessellated corridor which has subsided into the soft filling of an early ditch. Two burnt door-sills can be seen in doorways opening off this corridor.*

27a. *A mosaic of the same style as that in room 12 was laid in the southern part of the corridor in the second century.*

12. *The west wall of this room has been partially reconstructed. Some of the plaster from this wall has been restored in its original position.*

9. *This shallow grave cut through the pink mortar floor dates from some time after the building fell into ruins. The burial is one of several found on the site.*

10 & 11. *Second-century tessellated floors. Small patches of an earlier mosaic can be seen in room 11.*

11a. *The southern half of room 11 contains a mosaic panel with a central rosette enclosed within a central meander. This floor was laid after room 11 was subdivided at the beginning of the second century.*

13. *An early black and white mosaic overlain by a second-century polychrome mosaic. The ruts across the floor were gouged by medieval ploughing.*

32. *The second courtyard in the North Wing was completely destroyed during the Roman period. The position of the stylobate blocks which supported the colonnade and the stone gutter blocks have been marked by paving slabs and textured cement.*

16. *The superstructure of the eastern part of the building was demolished to ground level in the second century and many of the wall-foundations still survive.*

21. *An unusual early mosaic, designed in white tesserae set against a black and dark grey background. The white diamond in the south border may be the mosaicist's 'trademark'.*

19. *A first-century black and white floor with a simple pattern of overlapping rectangles.*

Remains of a bath suite built in the early second century:

24. Caldarium *or hot room.*

34. Tepidarium *or warm room with a small plunge bath (28).*

33. Frigidarium *or cold room with a drain built of reused gutter blocks.*

Trademarks and Signatures

Master craftsmen took pride in their work, and from an early period mosaic floors were signed. A pebble mosaic laid at Pella in Macedonia in the fourth century BC is signed by the artist Gnosis, and a floor laid at Pergamon in the second century BC has the signature of Hephaistion set against a simulated papyrus scroll made of tesserae. Many mosaic floors in Italy were signed by craftsmen with Greek names, and floors in Gaul are sometimes signed by artists with Latin names, evidence that skilled artists were commissioned to travel throughout the Roman Empire. A pavement from Lillebonne, in northern Gaul, is signed *T .Sen.c(ivis) Puteolanus Fec(it) Amor c(ivis) K(arthaginiensis) discipulus*, indicating that a master craftsman from Puteoli and a pupil from Carthage both worked on that mosaic floor.

The occurrence of inferior and highly skilled workmanship on the same mosaic floor suggests that master craftsmen and apprentices often worked side by side. For example, the head of Spring from the 'Four Seasons' mosaic found in Cirencester in 1849 is not as well drawn as the heads of Summer and Autumn in the same floor. The artist who created the head of Spring lacked any ability to use carefully graded colour shades to model the features, and the result is flat and expressionless. It is also noticeable that the boy on the dolphin in the central roundel of the Fishbourne mosaic is less well drawn than the supporting sea-beasts.

In Britain there are a few 'trademarks' on mosaic floors, and two of them occur at Fishbourne. The 'cupid on a dolphin' mosaic from the middle of the second century AD has a small bird motif inserted in the northern border which has no relevance to the overall design and must certainly be a trademark. On the first-century polychrome floor in room 21 there is a small diamond pattern in white tesserae, quite unrelated to the general scheme and therefore also a trademark. At the Roman villa at Bignor, a mosaic floor contains the cypher TER in a triangular panel, and this may possibly be the signature of a mosaicist named Terentius.

Top left: *A small bird 'trademark' inserted into a leaf and bud scroll border on the north side of the 'cupid on a dolphin' mosaic.*

Bottom left: *The cypher* TER *enclosed within a triangle on a fourth-century mosaic at Bignor, Sussex.*

Below: *The signature of the Greek artist, Hephaistion, written on a simulated scrap of papyrus. This is from a mosaic in the palace of King Eumenes at Pergamon dating from the second century* BC.

Marble and Stone Inlays

In the Roman Empire decorative marble and stone pavements and wall-decorations were usually made of tesserae; it was this technique that made the most economical use of stone. Sometimes however they were worked in *opus sectile*, using comparatively large pieces of stone, cut and shaped to fit the pattern. This technique has much in common with the techniques used by the Sumerian craftsmen who made composite inlays of stone and shell to decorate the Temple of Ninkhursag at Al'Ubeid.

Many of the Roman examples are abstract or geometric patterns composed of standardised elements of stone, shaped as triangles, lozenges rectangles, kites, *peltae* or circles. Later, wall-panels and pavements were made in Italy depicting elaborate figured scenes, and these panels were composed of individual elements cut and shaped to fit the picture. The craftsmen who made these figured panels must have worked from full scale 'cartoons'; the separate shapes would have been cut from templates made of wood, papyrus or parchment.

In Britain examples of *opus sectile* pavements or wall veneers are extremely rare, and Fishbourne provides the most complete evidence for their construction and use in this country. Several worn *opus sectile* elements were, however, found in the destruction levels of the Roman villa at Angmering, and, as this luxurious villa was constructed at approximately the same date as the Palace at Fishbourne, it seems possible that the same teams of craftsmen were used at both sites. Examples of individual *opus sectile* elements have also been found in London, Colchester, Chichester and Woodchester.

At Fishbourne a stone mason's workshop was established between AD 60 and 70. At this workshop *opus sectile* elements were cut and polished, architectural stone mouldings were made and tiny pieces of stone inlay were also produced for use on furniture. Unfortunately, none of the Fishbourne *opus sectile* pavements have yet been found *in situ*, but

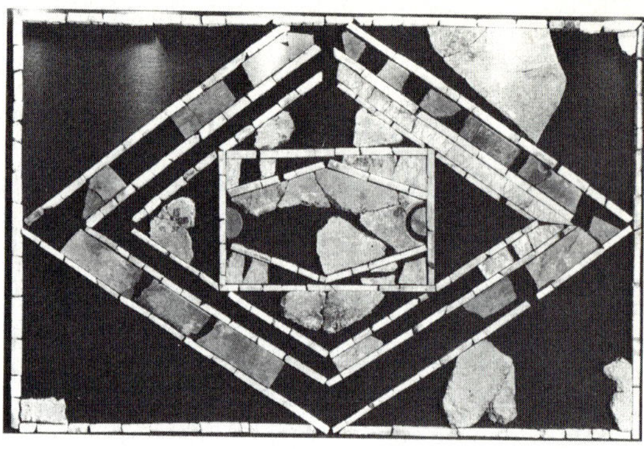

Above: *Reconstruction of a panel of marble wall veneer from the first-century palace at Fishbourne.*

Below left: *Excavation of a stone mason's workshop at Fishbourne, where stone was cut and polished for use in the proto-palace.*

Below: *Example of an* opus sectile *floor: many such floors still exist, particularly in Italy, though only marble 'elements' from them have been found in Britain.*

from the offcuts and rejected stone fragments left behind on the workshop floor it has been possible to establish the sequence of cutting and polishing operations.

The roughly dressed blocks of stone used in the workshop were brought by sea from Italy, France and the Isle of Purbeck. When the blocks arrived they were smoothed using a hammer or mason's mawl, and then cut into thin sheets. The technique of stone-cutting has been vividly described by the elder Pliny, and it seems that the techniques he describes in his *Natural History* are the same as those used by the Fishbourne craftsmen. The blocks were cut into sheets of varying thickness, according to the requirements of the end product. Thin sheets barely four millimetres thick were used for furniture inlays, while sheets twenty millimetres thick were required for pavements.

Many of the blocks were cut by multi-bladed iron saws using water as a lubricant and fine, sharp sand as the abrasive. These saw blades were probably suspended from an overhead pivot, since they would have been extremely heavy for even two men to handle. When the workshop was excavated three postholes were found cut into the floor and carefully lined with stone. These holes may have been the foundations for a tripod from which the heavy iron saw was suspended. No remains of the Roman saws have been found on the site, but clearly such valuable tools would have been dismantled and removed when the craftsmen finished working. However, the discovery of stone 'offcuts' with parallel saw-cuts clearly shows that multi-bladed saws were used.

After the stone had been cut into sheets, it was carefully smoothed with ironstone rubbers, and the required shape was marked out on the slab. Curved and circular elements were scored with a compass and a metal scribing tool, and then the shapes were cut out, with a fret-saw. Recent experiments have shown that it is possible to cut the stones used at Fishbourne with a hack-saw fitted with a stranded copper wire 'blade', provided plenty of sand and water are used as the cutting medium.

The straight-sided, geometric elements were marked out with a series of 'pecked' notches cut into the stone with a fine-pointed chisel. These notches provided the 'key' for a single-bladed toothless, iron saw which was used to cut the individual shapes. Many of the simple rectangular inlays were not cut completely through at this stage. A thin portion was left uncut and this could easily be snapped when the stone was required. The resulting 'burr' could be quickly smoothed off if necessary. It seems possible that the straight-sided elements were left joined together until needed by the artist working on the site. It would certainly have been far easier to store the elements as flat sheets than as random piles of separated blocks.

Archaeological evidence suggests that the inlays made in the Neronian workshop were used to decorate the proto-palace built in the sixties. No evidence has so far been found of the workshop which must have been in use when the Flavian Palace was built in AD 75.

Although no *opus sectile* floors have been found in the Flavian Palace, some of its walls were richly decorated with *opus sectile* panels and slabs of marble veneer. Many other walls were decorated with paintings simulating panels of vari-coloured marble inlay, and doorways and cornices were richly embellished with marble mouldings. One *opus sectile* panel in the North Wing remained in use for two hundred years until the building was destroyed by fire. During the fire the heavy marble inlays fell to the floor, where they lay in disorder until the archaeologists discovered them nearly nineteen hundred years later. Although it was impossible to reconstruct the panel accurately, it seems that the artist used strips of dull-coloured indigenous stones to enhance the clear brilliance of the imported marbles.

SED QVISQVIS PRIMVS INVENIT SECARE LVXVRIAMQVE DIVIDERE, INPORTVNI INGENII FVIT. HARENA HOC FIT ET FERRO VIDETVR FIERI, SERRA IN PRAETENVI LINEA PREMENTE HARENAS VERSANDOQVE TRACTV IPSO SECANTE... CRASSIOR HARENA LAXIORIBVS SEGMENTIS TERIT ET PLVS ERODIT MARMORIS MAIVSQVE OPVS SCABRITIA POLITVRAE RELINQVIT; ITA SECTAE ATTENVANTVR CRVSTAE.

Above: *The Elder Pliny was born in Como in* AD *23 and his 'Natural History' was published in* AD *77. In the extract quoted above, the author describes how marble was 'apparently cut by iron, but actually by sand, for the saw merely presses the sand upon a very thinly traced line, and then the passage of the instrument to and fro is in itself enough to cut the stone . . . .'*

Below: *A modern sculptor experimented in cutting stone using an iron blade, with sharp sand as an abrasive and water as a lubricant. Small notches were cut in the stone to give a 'key' for the iron blade and then the smooth blade was pushed gently to and fro with plenty of sand and water trickling into the groove from time to time. The stone cut easily with remarkably little effort.*

Floors at Fishbourne · 2nd generation

During the second and third centuries AD a series of new floor-mosaics was laid in the North Wing of the Palace. By far the most ambitious of these was the one laid in room N7 in about AD 150. Because of its almost perfect preservation, it is easy to appreciate the beauty of this mosaic, but all of the later series of mosaics at Fishbourne are technically and artistically inferior to those laid during the first century.

The general plan of the 'cupid on a dolphin' mosaic in room N7 was common in Britain and throughout the Roman Empire. It consists of a central circle supported by four semi-circles and four quadrants all enclosed within a square. This general arrangement is closely paralleled by the 'hunting dogs' pavement from a Romano-British town house excavated at Dyer Street in Cirencester and believed to date from the second century. The plan continued in use throughout the Roman period and can be seen again on the Christian pavement from Hinton St Mary, Dorset, now in the British Museum. All of the later floor-mosaics at Fishbourne are of an earlier date than most of those laid in Romano-British villas, although clear evidence is emerging of a 'spate' of mosaics laid on town sites in the latter half of the second century.

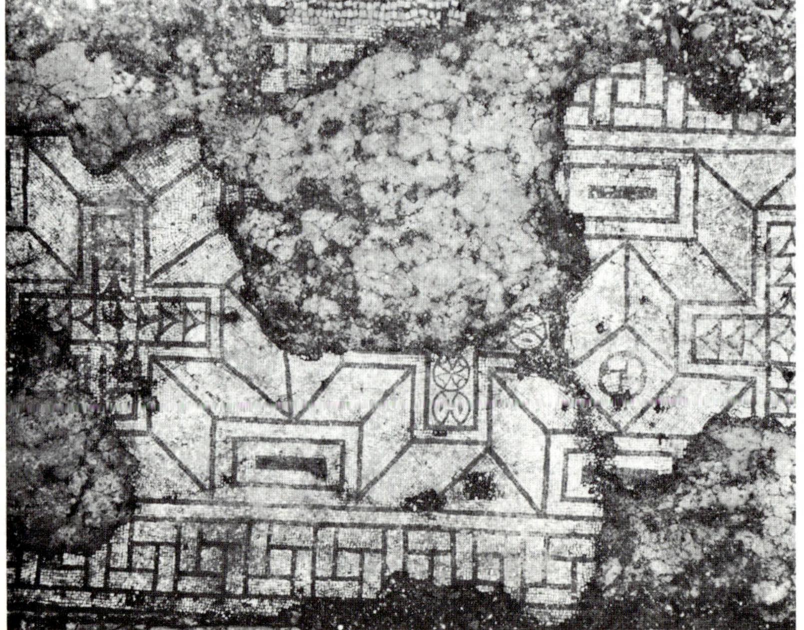

Above: *The polychrome mosaic in room N7 has many points of similarity with floor-mosaics found in the Mediterranean area. The division of the floor into circular, semi-circular and quadrant-shaped compartments, and the use of winged sea-horses in the semi-circular compartments, is paralleled in a floor from the Roman town of Salona (Yugoslavia), now in the Split Museum.*

Left: *The workmanship of the latest mosaic laid at Fishbourne in N8 is irregular and uneven. The central motif is a Solomon's knot set within a braided* guilloche *against a plain white background. On each side of the central roundel two dolphins cavort supporting a* cantharus. *The corners of the central panel are filled with radial fluting or 'scallop' pattern similar to that on the 'dolphin' floor in room N7. The simple border of diamond-within-rectangle motifs at each end of the mosaic panel, is similar to that found on a floor depicting Romulus and Remus from Aldborough in Yorkshire.*

Bottom left: *This mosaic floor was laid in the southern 'arm' of room N14 in the second century. At one time, this L-shaped room had served as a connecting corridor and the original floor was undoubtedly badly worn by the middle of the second century. The floor closely resembles the first-century mosaic in room N12, immediately to the west, which suggests it could be a copy. It is also possible that the worn floor was remade using the original tesserae.*

Right: *The arrangement of semi-circular panels around a central roundel in this floor has much in common with the plan of the fourth-century mosaic from Hinton St Mary (page 3) and with the 'lion and stag' mosaic from St Albans (page 30). The proportions and overall plan of the floor are excellent, but it is noticeable that the central figure of cupid seated on a dolphin is not as well drawn as the supporting sea-beasts.*

Top right: *The border of the floor-mosaic in room N7 is decorated with a foliate scroll emerging from a* cantharus.

Bottom right: *The central roundel on this second-century floor is set within a well executed, braided* guilloche *but the figures of the winged cupid and the dolphin are rather unskilfully drawn.*

Below: *The polychrome floor in room N13 at Fishbourne was laid over an earlier floor at the beginning of the second century.*

The workmanship of this floor-mosaic is crude; the colours are badly matched and it is obvious that the artist often had insufficient space to complete a motif properly. Nevertheless, the floor is interesting because it probably represents an early attempt by native craftsmen to work in a new medium.

The central motif of the head of Medusa is common in Roman art and was probably chosen from a 'pattern book'. The plan of the floor consists of a series of concentric squares, and the artist has linked the central square panel with the outer borders by six octagons containing stylised leaves, flowers and Solomon's knots, set against a chequer-board pattern background.

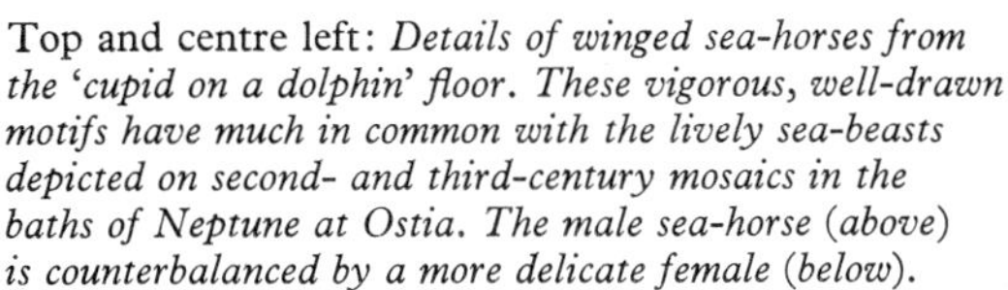

Top and centre left: *Details of winged sea-horses from the 'cupid on a dolphin' floor. These vigorous, well-drawn motifs have much in common with the lively sea-beasts depicted on second- and third-century mosaics in the baths of Neptune at Ostia. The male sea-horse (above) is counterbalanced by a more delicate female (below).*

Bottom left: *Detail of the head of Medusa from the mosaic in room N13. A portion of the underlying first-century mosaic can be seen beneath the Gorgon's head.*

Overleaf page 30

Top left: *This finely executed head of Medusa is from a fourth-century mosaic in the Bath Suite at the Roman villa at Bignor. By this late date there is evidence of several* officina *(workshops) working in southern Britain, and this* emblema *may have been prefabricated in a workshop and laid in position at the same time as the background. When this floor-mosaic was lifted recently it was carefully inspected for evidence of prefabrication; nothing conclusive was found, although examination of the reverse of the Medusa motif suggested that the irregularly shaped tesserae were too tightly and accurately set to have been laid by the 'direct' process.*

Top right: *The radial fluting or 'scallop shell' is also used in the corners of this floor in room N7.*

Bottom: *A second-century mosaic from a town house in Verulamium, St Albans. A growing number of second-century mosaics is now being recognised from urban sites in Roman Britain and this fine example from St Albans has much in common with the 'cupid on a dolphin' mosaic from Fishbourne. The arrangement of the central panel within a braided* guilloche *surrounded by semi-circular panels is similar in both floors and they both show a general high standard of background detail.*

Overleaf page 31

Top left: *Two important 'scallop shell' or fan-shaped motifs on each side of a central panel appear on this mosaic in room N5, which was probably laid at the same time as the 'cupid on a dolphin' floor. A major portion of the central panel has been destroyed, but the tails of two fishes can be seen at the edge of the worn area.*

Top right: *The eastern and western semi-circular compartments of the mosaic in room N7 show a pair of winged sea-panthers in carefully selected shades of red, yellow, white and black within a border of twisted* guilloche. *The 'male' panther appears to be more robust and is equipped with fangs and claws. The female is altogether more fragile with winged fore-hooves and no fangs.*

Bottom: *Scallop shell mosaic from Verulamium (St Albans) dating from the second century. The careful use of colour and shading on the flutes of this shell is the work of a fine craftsman. The shell is set against a plain background within a wave-pattern border.*

Other floors from Roman Britain

Unfortunately, there is no complete gazetteer of Romano-British mosaics available and the brief list which follows only attempts to direct attention to some of the more important mosaics which can be seen *in situ* or in a museum. Many of the earlier sites where mosaics were discovered are no longer open to the public, and in many cases the only record of a floor is a nineteenth-century drawing.

Woodchester, Gloucestershire. One of the largest and finest floor-mosaics in Britain, unfortunately only re-excavated and exhibited for brief periods every ten years. Three concentric pictorial friezes

Below: *Orpheus mosaic from Barton Farm, Gloucestershire (now in the Corinium Museum, Cirencester). The central roundel shows Orpheus seated and playing a lyre. He wears boots, a short tunic, a cloak and a Phrygian cap and he is surrounded by three concentric circular panels. The inner panel once contained a frieze of eight birds blissfully walking round charmed by the poet's music. Many of the figures are damaged beyond recognition, but two peacocks and a goose, or large duck, can still be identified. The outer panel originally contained a frieze of animals, but unfortunately only a lion, a leopard and a tiger survive.*

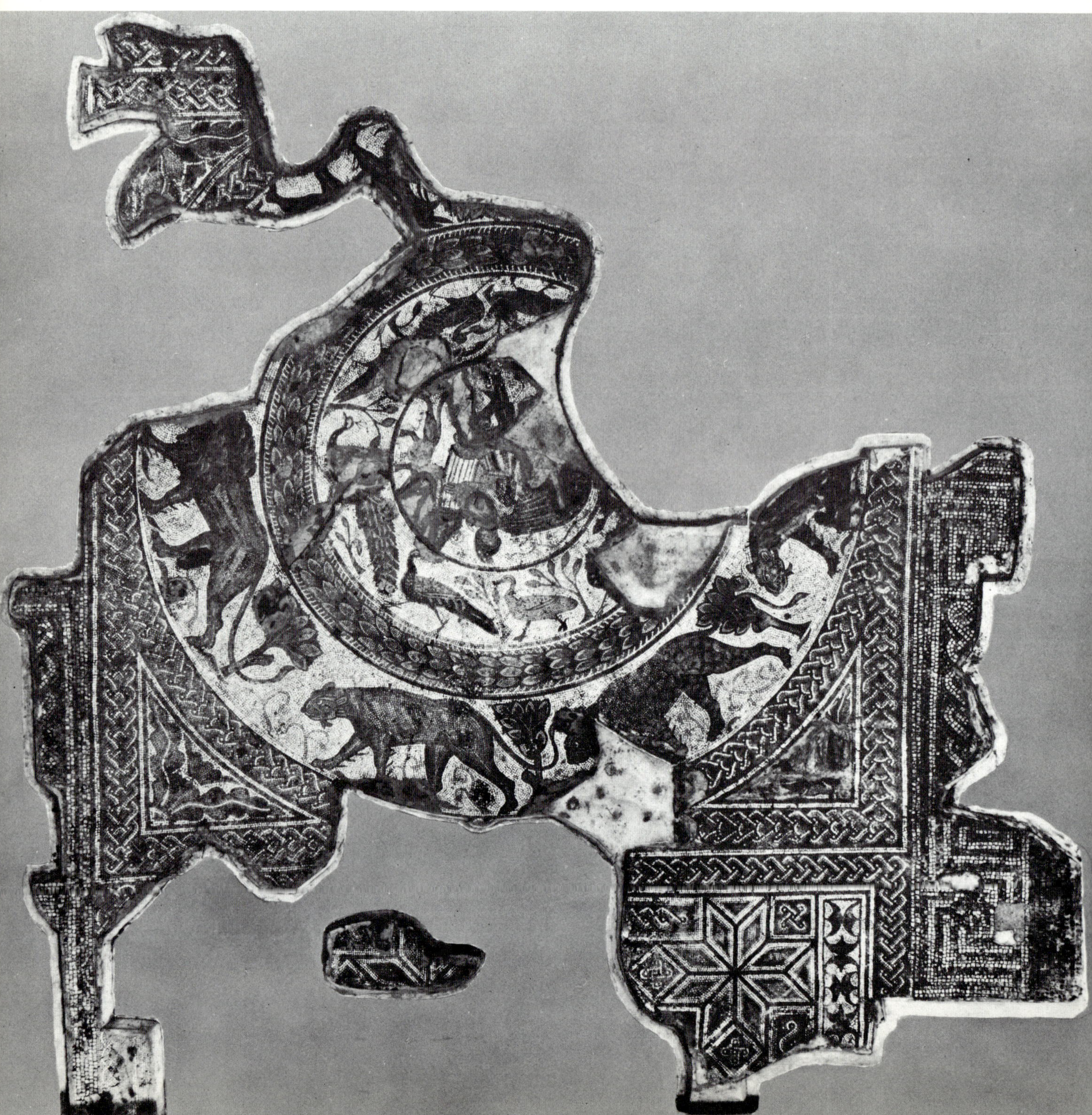

depict the legend of Orpheus and the beasts; many of the individual motifs in this floor are like those in floor-mosaics found at other sites in Gloucestershire. These Orpheus mosaics are thought to be the product of a school of mosaic workers operating in *Corinium* (Cirencester) in the third century AD.

Dyer Street, Cirencester, Gloucestershire. Mosaic with the four seasons in the corners (now in the Corinium Museum, Cirencester). Three of the seasons survive and each is represented by a bust of a young girl. Spring is crowned with leaves and flowers and has a flowering branch by her right shoulder, while a bird perches on her left shoulder; Summer wears a head-dress of ears of wheat and carries a sickle over her right shoulder; Autumn wears a chaplet of grapes and vine leaves and carries a pruning hook. Personification of the four seasons was a favourite theme of mosaicists all over the Roman Empire, and in Britain other fine examples occur at Bignor (Sussex), Brading (Isle of Wight) and Chedworth (Gloucestershire). Although the mosaic is badly worn, two other important roundels survive. One depicts the metamorphosis of Actaeon into a stag, the second shows Silenus with a wine cup in his hand riding in a precarious semi-reclined position on a donkey.

Barton Farm, Gloucestershire. Mosaic depicting Orpheus and the beasts (now in the Corinium Museum Cirencester). Concentric friezes of birds, garlands and animals surround a central *emblema* depicting Orpheus seated and playing the lyre. A similar pavement found in Dyer Street, Cirencester, but now destroyed, was undoubtedly made by craftsmen from the same workshop.

Lullingstone Villa, Kent. Important mosaic in the *triclinium* built in about AD 330 (*in situ* in villa open to the public). The main floor depicts Bellerophon riding the winged horse, Pegasus, and thrusting his spear at the Chimera. The legendary Chimera has a lion's head and serpent's tail, and the head and shoulders of a goat sprout rather unconvincingly from its back. The adjoining mosaic in the apse of the *triclinium* depicts Europa and the Bull and contains a tessellated metrical inscription referring to the first book of the *Aeneid*. The subject matter and the inscription throw a suprising light on the standard of literacy of the wealthy fourth-century villa-owner who commissioned the floor.

Bignor, Sussex. Four important fourth-century figured pavements (*in situ* in villa open to the public). The central *emblema*, in a floor in the bath suite depicting the finely drawn head of Medusa, may be prefabricated, since it would have been difficult to execute such fine motifs by the 'direct' process. Recent investigation of the mortar matrix beneath the floor failed to yield conclusive evidence. The apse in the *triclinium* contains a finely executed floor with the nimbed head of Venus supported on either side by a peacock perched on a leafy branch. The colours of the bird's feathers are enhanced by the use of glass tesserae. A narrow frieze running along the chord of the apse contains nine winged cupids dressed and armed as gladiators and practising under the supervision of cupid trainers. Another floor, which is largely complete, shows Ganymede being carried to Olympus by an eagle.

Low Ham, Somerset. Late fourth-century mosaic depicting the story of Dido and Aeneas (now in the Somerset County Museum, Taunton). The story from Virgil is told as a pictorial 'serial' in a series of well-drawn panels. Like the floor at Lullingstone, this mosaic throws light on the literary tastes and education of the villa-owner.

Hinton St Mary, Dorset. An important mosaic floor containing the head of Christ in the central *emblema* (now in the British Museum). Behind the head the Chi-Rho monogram clearly identifies the figure and in each corner there appears a male bust which may be interpreted as the four evangelists. These male busts appear to be

Top: *Mosaic from a Dorchester town house* (*now in the Dorset County Museum*). *Panel from a polychrome mosaic with a mask of Oceanus. Seaweed sprouts freely from the god's beard and his head is crowned with the legs of a crustacean. A floral scroll burgeons forth from each side of a central chalice in the border.*

Bottom: *Figured pavement from Chedworth, Gloucestershire, in the triclinium or dining-room* (in situ *in a villa open to the public*). *Four small dancing boys appear in the corners in the guise of the four seasons. Eight wedge-shaped panels around the central octagon contain Bacchic groups of satyrs and maenads.*

modified motifs usually used to personify the four winds; the awkward position of the right arm of each figure may indicate that 'bought in' motifs were modified on the site. In the adjoining annex the floor continues and the central roundel shows Bellerophon slaying the Chimera. This pagan legend of good triumphing over evil is not out of place on a mosaic in a Christian household.

Brading, Isle of Wight. An important series of representational subjects without parallel in Roman mosaics (*in situ* in villa open to the public). The complex themes of Gnosticism and allegorical symbolism imply that the villa-owner, who commissioned the floors, was thoroughly literate and highly cultured.

Winchester City Museum. Fragmentary portion of a fine mosaic floor from a town house, showing dolphins and geometric patterns.

Sparsholt, Hampshire. A geometric mosaic with an unusual 'floral chalice' in two corners (now in Winchester City Museum). The wine cup has a solid base and a band of jewels around its girth, but the top of the cup opens out as a half-opened flower bud with emerging tendrils.

Aldborough, Yorkshire. Unusual mosaic illustrating the legend of Romulus and Remus (now in Leeds City Museum). Although extremely naive in its execution, this floor is of interest since it illustrates an awareness of the time-honoured symbol of Rome on one of her farthest frontiers.

Below: *Detail from a cupid frieze which separates the Venus mosaic (page 7) from the main pavement in the* triclinium *at Bignor villa. The frieze contains twelve winged cupids; three are dressed as 'trainers' and nine play the parts of gladiators. The idea of illustrating scenes of everyday life with cupids as actors was popular in Pomeian wall-paintings and gladiatorial scenes were a favourite theme of mosaicists. In this detail a trainer, or* magister, *holding a* rudis, *or rod, to show he is a retired gladiator, is leading forward a* retiarius *clutching his net and trident, while a* secutor *prepares to fight by putting on his vizored helmet. The whole panel is a lively reflection on the romanised tastes of the owner of Bignor villa.*

Rudston, Yorkshire. (now in Kingston-upon-Hull Museum). One mosaic depicts a wild figure of Venus in a lively manner; four lunettes at the sides of the floor feature a lion, stag, leopard and bull. The lion and the bull are named in tessellated inscriptions. All of the figures are ill drawn, but they are redeemed by a native liveliness often lacking in more stereotyped mosaics. A second floor, lifted for conservation in 1972, has a perspective view of a triumphant charioteer holding aloft a victor's garland.

Leicester. (now in Leicester Museum). An octagonal panel found in the seventeenth century shows Cyparissus with his pet stag. Nearby a winged cupid waits to shoot his arrow at the youth. The missing portion of the floor may have illustrated the remainder of the legend where Cyparissus is transformed into a Cypress tree.

Verulamium. Several important mosaics from town houses (now in the Verulamium Museum, St Albans). Most notable is a great fan-shaped scallop shell, beautifully coloured and shaded by means of carefully selected tesserae. Among the other second-century floors, one portrays a large bust of Oceanus with well-drawn features and another shows a lion devouring a stag as its central motif supported by four chalices within a conventional framework of braided *guilloche.*

Below: *Three panels in a large floor-mosaic at Brading, Isle of Wight. In the centre of the rectangular panel on the right, a bearded astronomer is seated pointing with a rod at a globe while alongside him there is a sundial on a pedestal. The square panel in the centre is divided into four rectangular compartments, each illustrating some form of promise or fulfilment. In the upper right-hand panel, Ceres is shown giving Triptolemus ears of corn and a ploughshare before sending him to spread the cultivation of grain throughout the world. In the partially destroyed panel on the top left, a satyr pursues a maenad and in the lower left-hand panel Lycurgus is shown attacking Ambrosia with a double axe. In the lower right-hand panel, a shepherd boy holding Pan-pipes and a shepherd's crook stands rather stiffly alongside a maenad holding a tambourine. Below his short tunic, the shepherd boy wears a remarkable pair of short trousers which reach to his mid-calf. In the triangular areas between the panels there are busts of the four winds. The central panel contains an awesome Medusa set at an odd angle to the alignment of the room and to the panels of the mosaic. It may be that this motif was prefabricated and then carelessly set in position at the wrong angle. The centre of the rectangular panel on the left depicts a merman with two tails, one for each leg, and on each side of him a languorous Nereid reclines on the tail of a sea-centuar. The complex themes of bliss and rewards in the after-life which can be deduced from this mosaic are repeated on other mosaics at Brading and they give some idea of the cultured tastes of the villa owner.*

History of the Mosaic Floors

The first mosaic craftsmen arrived at Fishbourne between AD 60 and 70. They probably came by sea from the continent especially for this job, as it is unlikely that there were native mosaic craftsmen working in the Province at that early date. They arrived at a site which had been occupied by fairly cosmopolitan people since the earliest days of the Roman Conquest.

In AD 43, a group of buildings, linked by a well laid system of streets, was established by the side of the sheltered harbour at Fishbourne. These buildings were used as storehouses and granaries and were almost certainly part of a supply depot serving the needs of the Second Augusta Legion during its campaign in Wessex. As the front line moved forward, the supply base became redundant and in its place there developed a series of workshops and houses, forming part of a settlement which has been only partially excavated. At this early date, the site would have had much to recommend it to a property developer. It stood close to the shores of a safe, sheltered harbour, and it was well connected by road with the rapidly developing town of Chichester, a mile to the east. From Chichester, it was possible to reach London in two days, changing horses at posting stations along the route.

In the early 60s a major rebuilding programme was started. First the site was deliberately cleared and drained. Timber buildings were demolished and the clay from their clay-daub walls was spread over the low-lying part of the site. A network of major drainage ditches was dug, and the stream which formerly had flowed past the houses and workshops was diverted to the east of the site. Then a stone-mason's workshop was created where exotic marbles and other imported stones were cut and shaped for floor-tiles and furniture inlays. Finally, in the south-eastern corner of the site, close to the open waters of the harbour, an impressive house was built, its fine rooms richly decorated with wall-paintings and its floors surfaced with mosaic and *opus sectile*. This building may well have been the palace of the local client-king, Cogidubnus, who ruled the area after the Conquest.

Reconstruction of the proto-palace with its fine suite of baths.

Artist's impression of supplies being unloaded at the military depot soon after the invasion.

Artist's impression of the palace in AD 75 viewed from the east.

In about AD 75, a new building programme was begun and the site was again levelled and landscaped. Built on a series of terraced platforms, the Palace was thoroughly Italian in concept. The main building was designed as four wings of rooms around an open rectangular area laid out as a formal garden. The West Wing remained elevated five feet above the other three wings and the enclosed garden area. To the south of the Palace an artificial terrace was created by filling in the swampy, shallow water at the edge of the harbour and revetting the southern edge of this platform with solid oak piles driven into the harbour mud. Ships were able to sail right up to the southern terraced garden of the Palace, and undoubtedly paths and streets led directly to the main entrance hall.

Most of the rooms in the Palace were decorated with mosaic floors, and the use of a simple band of red brick tesserae around the edges of these early floors shows that they were laid before the walls were plastered and painted. In rooms 3 and 12 in the North Wing the mosaic floor can still be seen underlying the plaster, and even where the plaster had been totally destroyed, traces of mortar could be seen on the faces of these edging tesserae when the site was excavated. None of the later secondary floors have this edging of red brick tesserae.

After the first century there were several periods of rebuilding, and during the next hundred years several new mosaic floors were laid. At the end of the third century it seems that a new and ambitious rebuilding programme was just beginning when the building was swept by fire. After the fire, the ruins were searched for tiles and other building material which could be used again, and for a time the shell of the building was used as a 'quarry' for building stone. During the Saxon period the site became gradually concealed beneath a mantle of loam and vegetation and it lay completely forgotten until 1960, when a workman employed by the local water company cut a trench through two mosaic floors and several stone walls. Fortunately, the engineer in charge of the work called in local archaeologists, who realised the importance of the discovery. For the next eight years, a series of annual excavations was arranged and carried out under the auspices of the Chichester Civic Society Excavations Committee. Gradually the story of the site and its occupants was built up from the structural evidence of the different types of buildings and also from the rubbish discarded by the people who lived and worked at Fishbourne. The stone-mason who tossed aside his miscut pieces of marble left behind clear evidence of his working methods - something very difficult to determine from a perfectly finished piece of stone. The Palace servant who tipped rubbish into the muddy waters of the harbour could never guess how eagerly the twentieth-century archaeologist would seize upon the small objects of wood and leather fortuitously preserved in the mud.

It is from discoveries like this that the 'flesh' can be put on the 'bare bones' of evidence.

Several mosaic floors at Fishbourne remained in use throughout the life of the building - a period of two hundred years. Some floors were carefully repaired when they began to wear, while others were patched with mortar or clay. In room 12, the mosaic was repaired by an unskilled mosaicist, and in rooms 3 and 4 areas of wear were patched with a layer of pink mortar. Often these areas of wear reflect the passage of feet between doorways or in front of an oven.

At the east end of the North Wing several mosaic floors have slumped down into the soft organic fill of an early drainage ditch, and in rooms 20 and 21 the tesserae have gently subsided into the postholes of an early timber building. Because this subsidence took place gradually, there has been comparatively little lateral distortion of the mosaics.

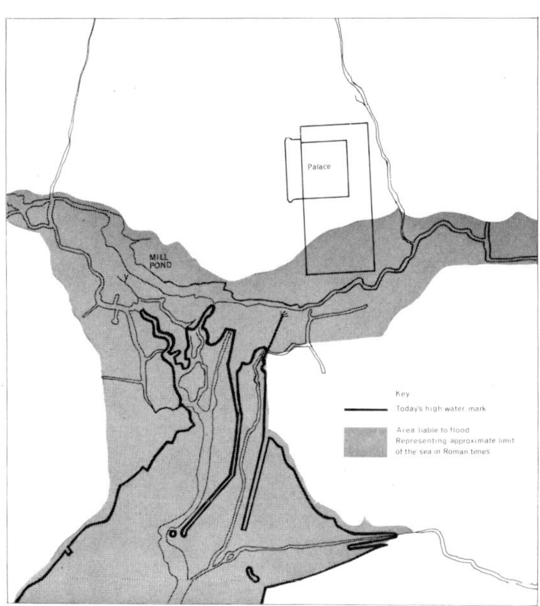

Above: *The Fishbourne site lies at the head of one of the inlets of Chichester Harbour where there is little to see today except low-lying marshes and creeks, drained by two small streams. In Roman times, before the creeks silted up, ships could lie safely in this sheltered anchorage while they waited to unload their cargoes.*

Below: *Several mosaic floors were very fragile when they were discovered. In order to preserve them they had to be consolidated; three were in such poor condition, with little adhesion between the tesserae and the Roman mortar below, that they had to be completely lifted and relaid.*

A stylised section through the stratified deposits at Fishbourne.

Three photographs taken when the mosaic floors were first excavated.

Top: *Cleaning the first area of mosaic found in 1961. This mosaic was lifted by volunteers and stored for nearly six years before it was returned to the site and relaid.*

Centre: *Removing the last layer of fine dirt and small stones from over the Medusa mosaic.*

Bottom: *General view of the excavation of the west end of the North Wing.*

After a few seasons of careful excavation, the site was purchased by the Sussex Archaeological Trust and a modern building was constructed over the North Wing. The walls and floors have been conserved *in situ* and one floor which was lifted in 1961 has been returned to the site and re-laid in its original position. In some rooms, the Roman mortar underlying the floor-mosaics was found to be badly decayed and it was necessary to lift these floors and re-lay them on a new foundation. Most of the floors, however, were in extremely good condition, and the tesserae were simply consolidated with a thin slurry of mortar brushed into the interstices.

Today, the floors are kept clean and free from algae and mosses. When they are freshly washed the colours of the natural stone are as clear and bright as the day they were laid. Because of the continual rising moisture from the subsoil beneath the floors, it is not advisable to seal the surface of the floors to enhance the colours. The maxim must be the same as that written in tesserae on a mosaic floor found at Torre de Palma in Portugal: *Sco(pa as)pra tessellam ledere noli uteri f(elix)* - 'Don't hurt the mosaic with a scratchy broom, but be careful of it.'

Mosaic Floors and Interior Decoration

Over a quarter of the villas discovered in Britain had at least one floor-mosaic, and it seems clear that wealthy Romano-British gentlemen demonstrated their material success by commissioning floor-mosaics for their country houses. Most of the floors laid in villas date from the late third and the fourth century AD, but before this floor-mosaics were laid in public buildings and also in the houses of wealthy businessmen. Clearly, a mosaic floor was a status symbol, and the fact that it was durable and easy to clean was probably of secondary importance.

Sometimes the scenes on the mosaic depicted the culture and education of the villa-owner - as in the case of the mosaic from Low Ham in Somerset, where a sequence of panels illustrates Virgil's *Aeneid.* This was hardly the type of floor to appeal to an uncultured British peasant.

Mosaics cannot be considered in isolation; they were only part of the room decoration, which often included wall-paintings and occasionally moulded cornices of stone, marble or stucco. At Fishbourne, many of the rooms with black and white geometric floor-mosaics were decorated with garish wall-paintings simulating panels of vari-coloured marble veneer. The most usual scheme included a dado about a metre high painted to represent red and pink veined marble. This was divided by a series of vertical black lines to increase the effect of marble panelling. Above the dado, black and white lines were used with coloured shading to simulate a moulded cornice and, above this, large 'panels' of marbling rose almost to ceiling height. This decoration may seem rather 'heavy' to modern eyes, but the rooms in which it was used were large and the marbled panels would have provided a strong contrast to the cool simplicity of the floor-mosaics.

Little is known about the wall decoration in the smaller rooms at the east end of the North Wing, where two early polychrome mosaics were laid. It is unlikely that the same scheme of simulated marble panels was used, as the effect would have been overwhelming in these small rooms. It is possible that a quantity of painted wall-plaster found in a dump to the west of the North Wing originally came from these rooms. This plaster is decorated with a yellow background, interrupted occasionally by foliage and rose-buds. On this background were painted panels representing alcoves and recesses and other pictorial views. One of the more important fragments shows a portion of a building set against a background of sea or sky. The painting is freely executed, the architectural detail and highlighting formed by a series of confident single brush-strokes. This distinctive impressionistic style was also used in a painting of a harbour scene at Stabiae in southern Italy. It cannot just be coincidence that two artists were painting similar scenes, using the same colours and the same distinctive style: this must be yet another example of continental artists working at Fishbourne in the first century.

Very little evidence survives of the furniture used in the rooms in Roman villas, but it seems that it was as grand as the architecture and the interior decoration. Several ornamental studs have been found, which were almost certainly used to fasten leather seats to the wooden framework of chairs or couches. A fine bronze handle formed by the cast figures of two dolphins probably came from a strong-box or a wooden chest, and a similar chest can be seen on the tombstone of Regina, now in South Shields museum. The wooden couches with thin mattresses from Herculaneum are well known and similar couches can be seen on Romano-British tombstones. A fragment of leather, tooled and embossed, with traces of gilding still adhering to the surface was found when the Temple of Mithras was excavated in London. Small fragments such as this provide a tantalising glimpse of the lavish fitments and furnishings that must have been in daily use at Fishbourne.

The fruits of wealth: a typical Roman dessert.

Moulded stucco from a frieze in the North Wing.

Artist's impression of a second-century room in the North Wing.

Mosaics Today

Today mosaics are commissioned and created all over the world, and the range of subjects and materials is wider than ever it was in antiquity. It is even possible for a modern 'do-it-yourself' enthusiast to buy prefabricated sheets of plastic and stone mosaic panels to decorate walls and small objects. The modern 'boom' began for the same reason as the invention of the cone-shaped mosaic elements in Iraq five thousand years ago - the desire to recreate impermanent wall-decorations in a more durable medium.

In the seventeenth century, a workshop was founded in the Vatican to produce copies of oil and fresco paintings in *smalti*, and today modern artists' cartoons are translated into ceramic, stone and *smalti* mosaics. Many modern public and commercial buildings are embellished with mosaic murals, and the medium is particularly successful when it is applied to abstract or 'pop' art. At a more homely level, the use of tile and mosaic veneers on the walls of grocers' and butchers' shops came to be synonymous with hygiene and cleanliness during the first half of the twentieth century. The modern housewife or hotel-keeper who has a *terrazzo* floor laid in the hall or kitchen is merely echoing the ancient need to live with beautiful, hard-wearing surfaces which require the minimum of maintenance.

A modern mosaic mural depicting the Judgement of Solomon. This was designed by David Brackston and made by Carter Contracting for the Law Courts in Poole, Dorset.